Seeing

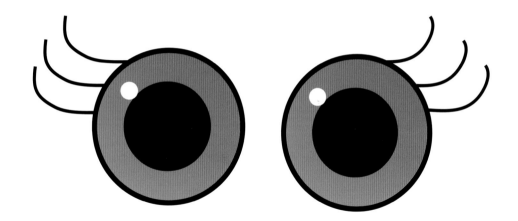

Katie Dicker

First published in paperback 2011,
by Evans Brothers Limited
2A Portman Mansions
Chiltern Street
London W1U 6NR

Produced for Evans Brothers Limited by
White-Thomson Publishing Ltd

Printed by Everbest in China
July 2011, job number (CAG1678)
Printed on chlorine-free paper from sustainably managed sources.

Educational consultant: Sue Palmer MEd FRSA FEA
Project manager: Katie Dicker
Picture research: Amy Sparks
Design: Balley Design Limited
Creative director: Simon Balley
Designer/Illustrator: Michelle Tilly/Andrew Li

The activities in this book are designed to be used at the discretion of the pre-school
practitioner, teacher or parent/guardian. The publisher shall not be liable for any
accidents, losses or malpractices arising from or relating to these activities.

British Library Cataloguing in Publication Data

Dicker, Katie
  Seeing. - (My senses) (Sparklers)
  1. Vision - Pictorial works - Juvenile literature 2. Visual
  perception - Pictorial works - Juvenile literature
  I. Title
  612.8'4

ISBN: 978 0 2375 4448 5

Contents

Different eyes

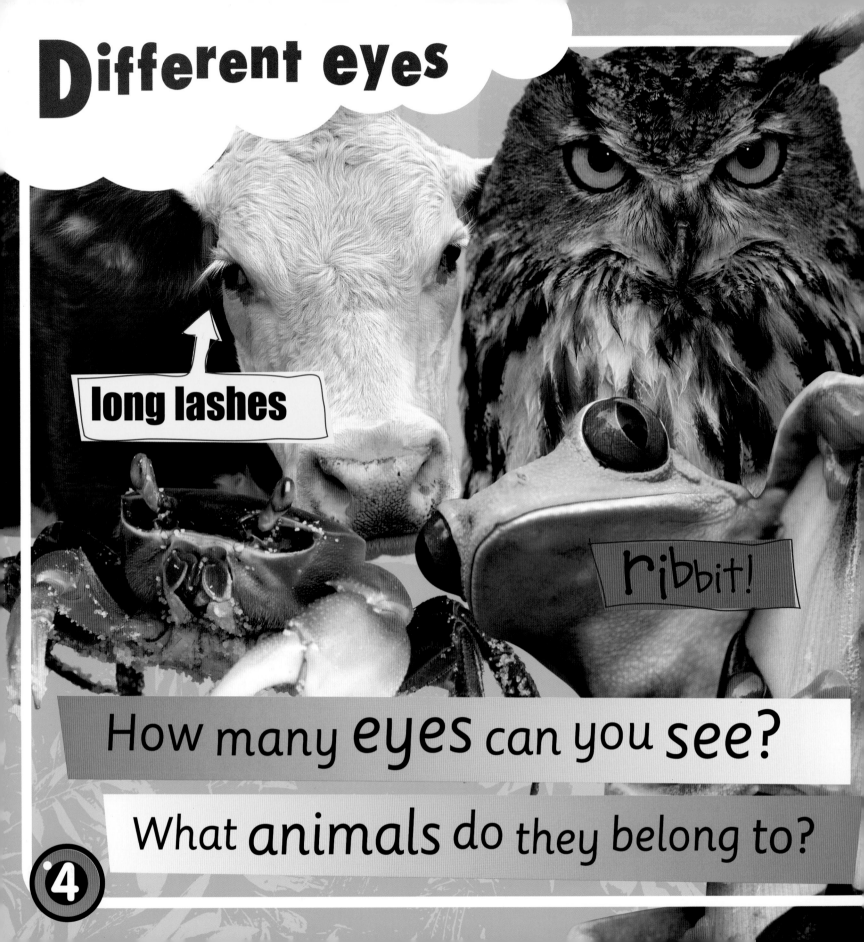

long lashes

ribbit!

How many eyes can you see?

What animals do they belong to?

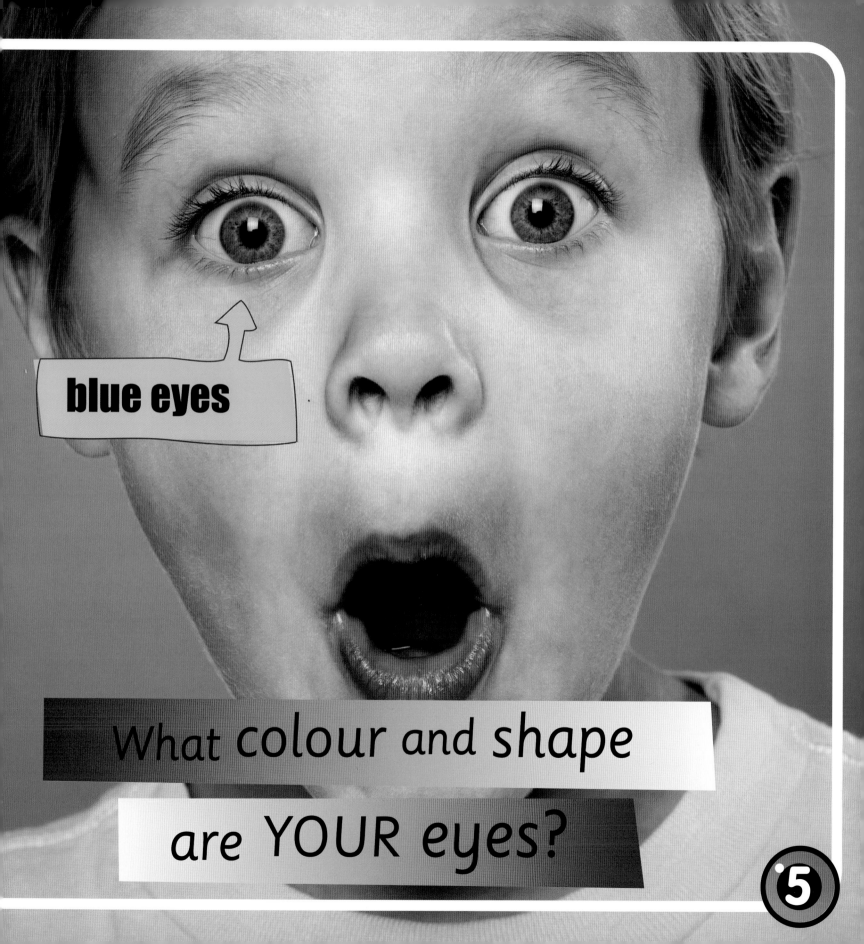

blue eyes

What colour and shape are YOUR eyes?

5

Sunlight

When the sun's out, we see things clearly.

Rainbow colours

I'm sinking!

These balls are brightly coloured.
Which colour do you like best?

8

What colours has Holly mixed to make green?

Light up the dark

We use lights to see when it gets dark.

A torch can help to show you the way.

Helping Us to See

Some people need glasses to help them to see.

Sunglasses **protect** our *eyes* in *bright* sunlight.

Near and far

magnifying glass

Get closer! What does a butterfly really look like?

This telescope helps us to see in the distance.

Mirror image

That's me!

We can see our reflection in a mirror.

jump!

Sometimes water reflects like a mirror, too.

17

Look out!

lighthouse

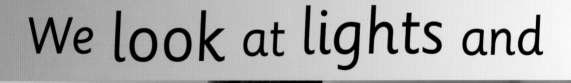
We look at lights and signs to keep us safe.

The colours of this frog tell other animals to stay away.

poisonous

19

Look again!

broken straw?

Sometimes our eyes play tricks on us.

Do **you** think these lines are straight or sloping?

Notes for adults

Sparklers books are designed to support and extend the learning of young children. The **Food We Eat** titles won a Practical Pre-School Sliver Award, the **Body Moves** titles won a Practical Pre-School Gold Award and the **Out and About** titles won the 2009 Practical Pre-School Gold Overall Winner Award. The books' high-interest subjects link in to the Early Years Foundation Stage curriculum and beyond. Find out more about Early Years and reading with children from the National Literacy Trust (www.literacytrust.org.uk).

Themed titles
Seeing is one of four **Senses** titles that explore the five senses of sight, touch, smell, taste and sound. The other titles are:

Hearing   **Tasting and Smelling**   **Touching and Feeling**

Areas of learning
Each **Senses** title helps to support the following Foundation Stage areas of learning:
Personal, Social and Emotional Development
Communication, Language and Literacy
Mathematical Development
Knowledge and Understanding of the World
Physical Development
Creative Development

Making the most of reading time
When reading with younger children, take time to explore the pictures together. Ask children to find, identify, count or describe different objects. Point out colours and textures. Allow quiet spaces in your reading so that children can ask questions or repeat your words. Try pausing mid-sentence so that children can predict the next word. This sort of participation develops early reading skills.

Follow the words with your finger as you read. The main text is in Infant Sassoon, a clear, friendly font designed for children learning to read and write. The labels and sound effects add fun and give the opportunity to distinguish between levels of communication. Where appropriate, labels, sound effects or main text may be presented phonically. Encourage children to imitate the sounds.

As you read the book, you can also take the opportunity to talk about the book itself with appropriate vocabulary such as "page", "cover", "back", "front", "photograph", "label" and "page number".

You can also extend children's learning by using the books as a springboard for discussion and further activities. There are a few suggestions on the facing page.

Pages 4–5: Different eyes
Children may enjoy making animal masks and cutting holes for their eyes to look through. Encourage children to look at books or magazines for ideas. Ask them to think about different types of animals and why they have the eyes that they do.

Pages 6–7: Sunlight
Explain to children the way the Earth rotates around the Sun and the pattern of day and night. Children may enjoy acting this out to aid their understanding. One child holds a lantern to represent the Sun. Another is the Earth moving around the Sun in a circle, while also rotating.

Pages 8–9: Rainbow colours
Ask children to mix paints together to make different colours. Encourage them to describe the colours they have made. Which are lighter? Which are darker? Which colour do they like best? What do the colours make them feel like? What objects in the world around them do they associate with each colour?

Pages 10–11: Light up the dark
Collect a series of magazines with photographs taken at night – for example car headlights, street lamps, neon signs, house lights or festival lights. Ask children to identify the different lights shown in the pictures. Encourage them to think about what these lights are used for.

Pages 12–13: Helping us to see
Children may enjoy designing their own pair of glasses using cardboard, felt-tip pens and decorations such as feathers or glitter. Children who already wear glasses could design a pair of sunglasses. Explain to the children why sunglasses are important.

Pages 14–15: Near and far
Show children how to use a magnifying glass, a telescope or some binoculars. Children may enjoy making their own telescope or binoculars using cardboard tubes. They could also draw pictures using a magnifying glass – ask the children to look at insects, or static objects such as the back of a leaf or a flower petal, through a magnifying glass and to draw what they see.

Pages 16–17: Mirror image
Take children on a walk and encourage them to look for their own reflection in different objects – such as metal objects, a window or a pond. Talk about why some objects (shiny/flat) reflect light better than others (dull/textured). Children may also enjoy drawing a self-portrait by looking at their reflection in a mirror.

Pages 18–19: Look out!
Talk to children about the visual warnings we use in everyday life, such as traffic lights, signs and level crossings. You could also encourage children to look at pictures of animals from wildlife magazines. Ask the children to think about why some animals are coloured in particular ways – such as warnings or camouflage.

Pages 20–21: Look again!
Fill a tray with ten objects, such as a cork, a pencil, a ribbon, a paperclip etc. Ask children to look at the tray for a minute and memorise the items they see. When you have removed one object, ask the children to write down which item is missing. You could also use the internet to find some simple optical illusions or magic tricks (see www.funology.com/abracadabra, for example). Ask the children to describe what they see.

Index

Picture acknowledgements:
Corbis: 6 (Ariel Skelley), 10 (Bryan Allen), 11 (William Gottlieb); **Getty Images:** cover, 13 (Dennis Welsh/UpperCut Images), 5 (Nicole Hill), 7 (David Young-Wolff/Photographer's Choice), 8 (Mel Yates/Taxi), 14 (Peter Mason/Taxi), 15 (Stuart O'Sullivan/Stone), 20 (Science Fraction); **IStockphoto:** cover sky, 2-3 sky, 22-23 sky, 24 sky (Judy Foldetta); **Photolibrary:** cover sand (Alan Kearney), 9 (Lee White/Flirt Collection), 12 (Randy Faris/Flirt Collection); **Rex Features:** 16 (Burger/Phanie); **Shutterstock:** 4, 15 (Brad Thompson), 17 (Mandy Godbehear), 18 (FloridaStock), 19 (Nicola Vernizzi).